MIDNIGHT ALARM

MIDNIGHT ALARM
The Story of
Paul Revere's Ride

BY MARY KAY PHELAN

Illustrated by Leonard Weisgard

Thomas Y. Crowell Company · New York

Designed by JUDIE MILLS

MANUFACTURED IN THE UNITED STATES OF AMERICA

L.C. Card 68-17080

ISBN 0-690-53638-0

4   5   6   7   8   9   10

TO MY NEWEST CRITIC
Kelly Anne Phelan

Contents

1 CARVING A SHEEP'S TOOTH   1

2 THE GATHERING STORM   11

3 SPY MEETING AT THE GREEN DRAGON   20

4 THE SUNDAY RIDE   36

5 A KNOCK AT THE DOOR   49

6 TWO LANTERNS TO HANG   60

7 STEALING ACROSS THE CHARLES   68

8 BRIEF STOP IN CHARLESTOWN   77

9 NEAR-CAPTURE   84

10 MISSION COMPLETED   93

11 "HALT!"   102

12 "IF THEY MEAN TO HAVE A WAR"   112

    BIBLIOGRAPHY   121

    INDEX   125

MIDNIGHT ALARM

I

CARVING A
SHEEP'S TOOTH

Something is in the wind. Exactly what, no one knows. But there have been rumors and more rumors spreading through the narrow crooked streets of Boston all week long.

The date is Saturday, April 15, 1775. In his little shop at the head of Clark's Wharf, Boston's best-known silversmith is seated at his worktable. Paul Revere is a stocky man of forty with thick black hair and brown eyes. His friends admire his keen mind, his air of quiet determination. He does not frighten easily, they say. On many occasions these past few years he has shown great courage. In fact, he has been nicknamed "Bold Revere."

For twenty-seven years, "from sun-up to sun-down," this neat wooden building facing Fish Street has been Paul Revere's place of business. He grew up in the silversmithing trade, starting as an apprentice to his father, Apollos Rivoire, when he was thirteen. The family name had been changed not long after the father settled here in 1716. People of Boston found the French *Rivoire* very hard to pronounce, so Apollos had shortened it to Revere.

This morning there is no odor of burning willow charcoal from the brick furnace in one corner of the shop. The iron crucible used for melting down old silver coins is empty. The silversmith in his leather apron is no longer hammering out the silver bowls, the tankards, and the trays that have been the pride of Boston residents. No one has money to pay for such fine things these days. For the last few years Paul Revere has had to find other ways of making a living for his wife and six children.

First he taught himself how to engrave copperplates. These engravings often took the form of political cartoons, which the people of Boston enjoyed. From the copperplate he printed pictures that sold for a few pennies apiece. Revere was not an expert. There were others who made better engravings. But when times are hard, even a few pennies count.

Revere's most successful venture, however, has been the making of false teeth. This secret he learned from an Englishman, John Baker, in 1768. In Revere's time, there were no dentists in Boston. If a tooth ached badly, it was pulled out. And if the tooth happened to be a front one, the patient was left with a gaping hole in his smile.

No wonder that many have welcomed Mr. Revere's newest trade. His square hands with the blunt fingers became highly skilled in fashioning false teeth, which he himself would wire into the mouth of his patient.

At first Paul Revere used both ivory from the tusks of the hippopotamus and sheep's teeth to carve out false teeth. But lately it has become impossible to obtain any ivory from Africa. Actually, sheep's teeth are more regular in form, and people seem to like them better anyway.

This morning Revere takes out his tools and selects one of the animal teeth from his worktable drawer. He must be especially careful today. This tooth is for his good friend Dr. Joseph Warren. People have sometimes thought it strange—the friendship that has grown strong between these two men with such diverse backgrounds. Dr. Warren is six years younger than Revere, a graduate of Harvard College and a successful doctor. Most of his patients are wealthy citizens who live on Beacon Hill.

As the silversmith begins carving the sheep's tooth, his wide brow is wrinkled with worry. Something is about to explode in his beloved town. There is sure to be a clash with the British soldiers. But how and when will it start?

The trouble that is threatening is not something new. It began more than twelve years ago—right after the French and Indian War ended in 1763. The victorious British had driven the French out of Canada. But war is an expensive business. Although England now possessed a powerful empire in North America, there were many debts. King George III and his ministers decided the American colonists must be taxed to help pay for the war.

It was now more than one hundred and fifty years since the first Englishmen arrived in America. During this time the colonists had managed their own affairs with little or no interference from Britain. Now they resented the idea of paying taxes at the bidding of a king three thousand miles away.

"We're Englishmen, too," they said. "And we have the right of all Englishmen to have our representatives decide how we shall be governed and taxed."

Messages were sent to King George. The colonists asked permission to send representatives to Parliament—that group of officials in England who made the laws and decided about the taxes. King George would not hear of such a thing. The American colonies belonged to Britain, he said. Therefore, the colonists MUST pay whatever taxes the Parliament levied upon them.

Paul Revere remembers well that first tax. It was called the Stamp Act. All newspapers, all business papers, were required to bear a stamp. Otherwise, the business would not be legal. More taxes followed—taxes on molasses, sugar, and tea. The colonists were furious.

"It's taxation without representation," they said, "and taxation without representation is tyranny."

As the years passed, the quarrel with England became steadily worse. However, all people did not think alike. They began to divide into two groups—the Tories and the patriots.

The Tories were those colonists who were still loyal to the government of George III.

They had no objections to paying taxes as the Crown directed. They liked the idea of the colonies' being a part of the powerful British Empire. But the patriots, or Whigs as they were sometimes called, were bitter about having to pay taxes imposed by England.

The patriots held meetings at which they urged everyone to stop buying anything from England that was taxed. Most people agreed. Before long, trade between the two countries had practically halted.

English merchants became seriously alarmed. Much of their income depended on the goods they shipped to America. They were losing money rapidly. Finally, in December 1770, George III and Parliament decided to lift all taxes—except one very small tax on tea. The king and his ministers hoped to make the colonists forget that they were being taxed—without representation.

But the patriots were not to be fooled. They simply refused to buy tea from England. Either they drank tea smuggled in from Holland, or they went without. If people bought the tea from England, the patriots argued, they would be admitting that the king had a right to tax them.

At the moment the tax on tea was only a few pennies. Yet how could anyone be sure that more taxes might not again be added? Perhaps it would be a tax on their farms next —and then their fishing boats, their cargo ships, their shops. Who could tell where this taxation might end? It was better not to drink tea at all.

In Boston one of the patriot leaders, Samuel Adams, realized very early that a clash with the mother country would surely come. The shabbily dressed Adams is not a good public speaker. Quietly but effectively he has worked behind the scenes. He has written hundreds of letters, talked with thousands of people, urging resistance to British authority.

Paul Revere recalls that it was Sam Adams who organized "the Sons of Liberty." When gangs of young men from Boston's North End began fighting with gangs from the South End of town, Adams saw a great opportunity. He persuaded these high-spirited young men to join together in a secret organization. Under Adams' direction the Sons of Liberty have done everything possible to make life miserable for the British officials who were trying to carry out the king's orders.

It was Adams, too, who persuaded the town's wealthiest citizen, John Hancock, to join the patriots. Everyone thought that Hancock would surely side with the Tories. But Sam Adams convinced the tall handsome merchant that only freedom from England would secure the colonists' rights.

Confident that Adams is right, Hancock has given generous financial support to the cause and now devotes most of his time to working for independence. John Hancock and Sam Adams are known throughout Massachusetts Bay Colony as the leaders of the patriot movement, while Dr. Warren directs patriot activities in Boston.

2

THE GATHERING STORM

This morning the clump of army boots on the cobblestones of Fish Street reminds Paul Revere that it was only a little more than a year ago that the serious struggle really started. The details of that night of December 16, 1773, are still vivid in his memory. Three ships from London—the *Dartmouth,* the *Eleanor,* and the *Beaver*—sailed into the port of Boston loaded with chests of tea.

The arrival of the ships infuriated many of the citizens. Mass meetings were held. The patriots were determined that this tea should never reach their wharves. If the tea chests were unloaded, it would be admitting that

11

England had the right to tax the American colonists.

Sam Adams and John Hancock along with Paul Revere himself recruited fifty members of the Sons of Liberty. Their mission was to board the ships and throw the chests into the harbor. Behind locked doors on that night of December sixteenth, the raiders wrapped themselves in blankets, smudging their faces with soot and red paint. It was agreed they would be "Mohawks." When the secret signal was given, the raiders raced through the streets, yelling with excitement: "To Griffin Wharf!" "Boston Harbor a teapot tonight!"

Led by Adams, Hancock, and Revere the three groups of "Indians" stole aboard the ships. They had been carefully instructed not to take one leaf of tea for themselves. Everything must be dumped into the water—otherwise the "tea party" would be a robbery, not a protest against the king and his tax.

The "Mohawks" worked swiftly. Not a word was spoken aloud. When conversation was necessary, the men talked in Indian grunts. It took several hours to break open the heavy chests and pour the tea into the swirling waters below.

But not one thing was disturbed on the ships except the tea. After the "Indians" had finished their job, they borrowed brooms and swept up the decks. No one could ever say that the Boston Tea Party had been the work of a wild mob.

Everyone knew that the king would be angry. The punishment inflicted upon the colonists, however, was greater than anyone had imagined. On May 10, the British ship *Lively* brought the news. After June 1, 1774, no ship or boat could enter Boston Harbor. The port was to be closed until the people of Boston paid for the tea.

To a town that depends almost entirely on the sea for its commerce and trade, this was drastic news indeed. The citizens were stunned. Everything came by boat. Businesses would be ruined—the merchants depended

on the cargo for their shops. The seamen, the sailmakers, the fishermen would have no work. But even more terrifying would be the lack of food and fuel.

Boston was practically ringed by water. Only one small strip of land, called Boston Neck, connected the town with the rest of the colony. To close the harbor meant almost certain starvation.

On this morning of April 1775, Paul Revere well remembers the long horseback ride he was asked to make to New York and Philadelphia last May. As soon as the king's terrible edict was known, the Committee of Safety asked Revere to carry the news to the patriots in those towns. By the time he returned, four thousand British soldiers were quartered in Boston. Under the command of General Thomas Gage, these red-coated British regulars were to see that no boat entered Boston Harbor.

Up to this time, each of the thirteen American colonies had thought first of its own people. None of them paid much attention to their sister colonies. The king knew they were not united. He counted on this when he dealt out the harsh punishment. But George III was mistaken. The closing of Boston Harbor united the colonies as nothing had ever done before.

From all over the country food was hauled across Boston Neck into town. Wagons brought sacks of rice from South Carolina, bags of wheat from Maryland. Nearby Massachusetts towns sent rye, flour, and great quantities of salt codfish. Sometimes herds of sheep and cattle were driven across the quarter-mile width of land leading into Boston. The town did not starve. There were times when many were hungry, yet no one wanted to give in to the king's demands.

This morning as he carves out the tooth for Dr. Warren, Paul Revere feels a surge of pride for the courage the patriots have shown. It's been difficult, having four thousand soldiers quartered among Boston's fifteen thousand people, soldiers who strutted up and down the streets watching every movement the townspeople made.

This past winter was fairly quiet though—only occasional scuffles between citizens and soldiers. The children enjoyed taunting the redcoats. Behind their backs they chanted:

"Lobster-back, lobster-back
You're going to lose your claws."

Then the youngsters would scamper down the crooked alleys, leaving the redcoats more irritable than ever. Townspeople, too, pestered and insulted the soldiers constantly. But Paul Revere is thankful there was no exchange of gunfire.

Now, however, it's spring, and rumors are rampant. Tempers can flare at any moment. What is more, the British officers are daily drilling their men on Boston Common. Surely General Gage must be planning something. But what—and when and where?

Revere finds reassurance in the fact that the colonists have not been idle. Behind locked doors people are casting bullets. Pewter spoons, porringers, and teapots are being melted down into lead. And homemade gunpowder is concocted by grinding charcoal, sulphur, and saltpeter into a paste.

In every town and village throughout the Massachusetts Bay Colony, men are drilling. A number of men from each militia company have volunteered to be ready to fight

"at a minute's notice." These are the minutemen who day and night have their guns, bullets, and powder horns within easy reach.

Ammunition and food supplies are being
stored in secret hiding places all over the
colony. Most of the people realize that some
day they will have to fight England in order
to obtain their rightful liberties.

It is late afternoon now, and the silversmith
holds the false tooth at arm's length, survey-
ing his work. It is finished, and it looks quite
real. Tonight he will deliver it to Dr. Warren
after the meeting at the Green Dragon Tavern over in Green Dragon Lane. Perhaps he
will have more definite news to report to his
friend.

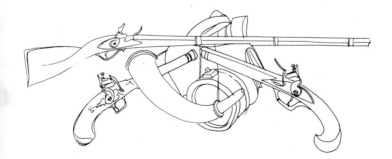

3

SPY MEETING AT THE GREEN DRAGON

Daylight is beginning to fade as Paul Revere locks the front door of his shop. Glancing out toward the harbor, he sees only the British patrol boats making their way slowly through the water. The twenty-four-hour-a-day watch is very efficient. For more than nine months now, nothing has come into Boston by way of the harbor.

The once bustling waterfront is strangely quiet. Revere misses the old familiar smell of fish drying along the wharf. The thump of handlooms in the sail-making shops, the whine of wooden machinery—these are sounds one no longer hears.

As Revere crosses Fish Street, he notes that the cobblestones are in good repair. This is one of the very few benefits that has come from King George's closing of Boston Harbor. It all started when the sister colonies began sending food to the starving town. There must be some fair way to distribute the bread, the meat, the flour. Boston selectmen, the gentlemen who controlled the town's affairs, decided to initiate work projects for the hundreds who had lost their employment.

Docks were cleaned and wharves repaired. Broken or crumbling cobblestones on the main streets were replaced. Even the twisting alleys were paved with pebbles which had washed ashore, some as large as goose eggs. People had to work for the food they received. There were plenty who grumbled, but their families needed the food desperately. The past few months have not been easy, but at least the town is clean as never before.

The silversmith threads his way through the British soldiers standing in small groups along the street. Fortunately his home on North Square is not far from his shop. With that meeting tonight at the Green Dragon Tavern, there is no time to lose.

Revere's face lights up with pleasure as his neat two-story frame house comes into sight on the west side of North Square. He bought the house from Captain Erving just five years ago—a house that was already one hundred years old. There's a parlor and kitchen on the ground floor with bedrooms above. Now everyone sleeps upstairs, a welcome change after the many years in the crowded house next to his shop on Fish Street.

North Square is a good place to live, too— though no one understands why it is called North Square. It is actually a triangle in shape, a piece of land where Prince, Sun Court, Garden, and Moon Streets all come together.

The triangular Square is bordered by houses and shops, built right up to the brick footway. Shopkeepers have signs denoting their trades

for those who have not yet learned to read. There's a large pair of scissors above a tailor shop. A gold lamb denotes a wool weaver's shop, and a huge painted book is the sign for a bookbinder.

Both householders and shopowners keep their small-paned windows sparkling. Brass door knockers are polished to a brilliant shine. Everyone is proud of the clean, well-kept appearance North Square presents.

There is always a bustle of activity around the Square. And Revere's wife, Rachel, appreciates the convenience of having the town water pump and the public market placed just across from the house. Bells seem to ring here all day long, too—shop bells, market bells, the bell of the town crier. Not far away is Christ Church with its sweet clear-toned bells that boom on special occasions.

When the British troops arrived in Boston last summer, most of them camped in tents down on the Common. Some were billeted in warehouses and barracks about town. But when winter set in, places of greater warmth had to be found. Parliament passed the Quartering Act which gave authority to order every family with a spare room to house one or more soldiers. The townspeople hated the idea, yet there was no way to refuse. Revere is thankful he has no extra room, although British officers are quartered all around him in North Square.

Revere's children have just finished a game in the spacious back yard when the silversmith enters his home. His little lambs, as he calls the youngsters, come quickly when they hear their father's voice. He is sorry, he tells them, but there will be no stories tonight. Just a quick bite, and he must hasten off. Only Rachel knows where he is going. The location of the meeting cannot be revealed, even to the children.

After a skimpy supper—there never seems to be enough to eat these days—Revere slips out the front door into the darkened street. Reaching into the pocket of his leather breeches, he makes certain he has the small box with Dr. Warren's new false tooth.

Revere walks slowly, so as not to attract the attention of any of the British soldiers loitering around the Square. Those infernal soldiers—they seem to be everywhere. The Green Dragon is not far, but he must be certain he is not followed. Tonight's meeting of his "Committee of Thirty" is too important to be endangered.

Last fall when so many were out of work, Paul Revere recruited thirty of his closest friends from the Sons of Liberty. He described them as "chiefly mechanics," men who had not worked since the closing of Boston Harbor. With these friends the silversmith organized a spy system—something yet unknown in the colonies. Years later Revere would write: "We formed ourselves into a committee for the purpose of watching the movements of the British soldiers and gaining every intelligence of the movement of the Tories."

The spy ring worked well. Day and night, all through the winter and early spring, the patriot spies patrolled the streets of Boston. Working always in pairs, chatting as they sauntered along so as not to arouse suspicion, they watched the British soldiers constantly —what they did, where they went. Anything unusual was immediately reported to Paul Revere. In turn, he passed along the messages to the patriot leader, Dr. Warren.

There were other ways, too, of learning what the British were plotting. Occasionally a redcoat became dissatisfied with army routine. He liked what he saw of the American colonists so he would merely "disappear" to settle down out in the countryside. If he were caught, he would be shot as a deserter, but a large number of redcoats became colonists overnight and gladly gave Revere's spies important information.

Striding through a dark alley near Hanover Street, Revere cannot help but smile. It was his spies who had uncovered what General

Gage was plotting last February. The British, they discovered, were planning to send reinforcements to the fort at Portsmouth, New Hampshire.

Revere had reported the plot to Dr. Warren immediately. The Portsmouth patriots must be warned, said the doctor, so Revere had volunteered. He saddled his horse and rode sixty miles over ice-covered roads to take the news. Minutemen sprang into action. The British fort was seized and a large amount of gunpowder captured before the hated redcoats ever left Boston. That one incident alone made the spy system worth all the effort.

On this Saturday evening of April fifteenth many of the men are already seated around the long table in the second-floor meeting room of the Green Dragon. When Revere enters, he places his hand on the Bible near the door and repeats the solemn oath each member must take as soon as he comes into the room. Secrecy is of the utmost importance. In taking the oath, each man swears on the

Bible that he will never repeat anything that occurs in the meeting.

Tonight the room fairly tingles with excitement.

One member reports that two young British officers, Captain Brown and Ensign de-Berniere, have been seen walking through nearby villages, "disguised as countrymen." Captain Brown pretended to be a gunsmith. He even repaired a gun for one of the farmers. These same officers have also been seen making sketches of the various towns, noting locations of bridges, churches, and shops. However, adds the spy, it was in the town of Concord that the officers asked the most questions.

The Committee of Thirty is well aware that Concord is the town where the patriots' largest military stores of gunpowder, cannon, flour, and lead are hidden. Several members wonder if perhaps General Gage has discovered their hiding place.

Everyone in Boston knows that early this

spring Parliament ordered Gage to seize any stores of arms and ammunition that the colonists may have hidden. Rumor has it that Gage believes that without ammunition the colonists would never try to resist. The British commander is determined to find the ammunition. Tonight's report would certainly indicate that General Gage strongly suspects the hidden stores are in Concord.

Another member reports that the British grenadiers and light infantry troops seem to have been taken off duty. These are Gage's picked troops. The grenadiers are chosen for their height and strength—heavy duty troops, they are called. The soldiers of the light infantry are bold, fast, and especially daring in small skirmishes.

There's also something further to report. Maybe it is even more significant. Several members who were patrolling along the waterfront this week saw boats from British transports being hauled up on the beaches and repaired. After being recaulked, they were returned to the battleships, ready for future action.

At this moment the door is flung open, and one of the spies dashes breathlessly up to Revere. Then he remembers he has not yet taken the oath, and he hurries back to swear upon the Bible before he explains his excitement. It is only minutes ago, he says, that he saw those small British boats, hundreds of them, being taken down from the transports and put into the water near Boston Common.

This is news, indeed—important news. Revere knows he must go to Dr. Warren's house at once. The meeting is quickly disbanded, although not before the leader utters a reminder of the oath each man has taken on the Bible. The spies must not reveal anything they have seen or heard this evening.

Fortunately Dr. Warren's house in Hanover Street is not far from the Green Dragon Tavern. Revere slows his steps, trying to seem as if he is going nowhere in particular. There are always British spies. You can never tell when you are being watched—or followed.

Knowing the shortcuts, Revere crisscrosses through the maze of twisting streets and alleys. Before many minutes have passed, he is at Dr. Warren's front door. The popular physician is just saying good night to his last patient. Though outwardly calm, Revere can scarcely wait to talk to his friend.

The news of the British soldiers making sketches of Concord, the report of the launching of the boats—it all fits together like the pieces in a puzzle. After hearing the details, Dr. Warren tells Revere he is sure the British are planning to march on Concord to capture the supplies hidden there.

Concord is the rallying point for the patriots. For many weeks carts filled with straw had rolled into the town. Boxes packed with cartridges and large cannon balls were hidden beneath the straw. Ten six-pound cannons are now stored at the Town House. A gunnery expert is teaching a special detail of men how to handle the cannon.

There's a danger, too, that the enemy has discovered the whereabouts of Sam Adams and John Hancock. Last October after General Gage dissolved the Massachusetts General Court, its members secretly formed the Provincial Congress. Adams and Hancock are the leaders of this congress, a group of patriots whose primary purpose is to promote the movement for independence. The Provincial Congress ended its session in Concord last Thursday. Hancock and Adams, knowing Gage considers them traitors, decided not to return to Boston. Instead, they are spending a few days with the Reverend Jonas Clark in Lexington. But the news tonight indicates the British may be planning to seize these patriot leaders.

Dr. Warren can see only one course of action to take. Tomorrow Revere must ride over to Lexington to warn the leaders. The British officers, if they get their hands on Adams and Hancock, could send them to London to be tried for treason. They could even be hanged.

This must never happen. The two men will soon be leaving for the Second Continental Congress in Philadelphia. It is here that Hancock and Adams hope to persuade their sister colonies to band together in the fight for independence. These leaders are much too important to the patriots to take any risk with their lives.

And those stores of ammunition at Concord. The doctor frowns. The hiding places must be changed at once. If General Gage seizes the carefully hoarded gunpowder, there will be nothing with which the patriots can defend their rights.

Dr. Warren urges Revere to ride on to Concord tomorrow, also. He should alert Colonel James Barrett of the coming danger. The word must be quickly passed if the patriots are to save their precious military stores.

Put on a good show, the doctor advises. Make it a leisurely ride. Stop and visit along the way. Don't gallop at a fast gait—simply saunter through the towns. If there are any

British soldiers lurking about, they must never suspect the real purpose of this Sunday ride.

The silversmith nods. He understands his instructions. And, by the way, here in this box is the tooth for Dr. Warren. He will wire it in later.

Warren nods absentmindedly. His thoughts are far away from dentistry at this moment. He shakes hands with his friend and wishes him luck.

As Revere walks back toward North Square, he reviews the plans for tomorrow. He must start early, slip out without being seen—before daylight, if possible.

4

THE SUNDAY RIDE

The first streaks of dawn have not yet appeared on the eastern horizon when Paul Revere sets out from his home on North Square. His early departure is deliberate. One never knows when the British are watching. And he doesn't want to be seen leaving town on this early Sunday morning.

After returning from Dr. Warren's last night, Revere decided that the best way to carry out his mission was to row across the Charles River. Trying to leave town by riding across Boston Neck might arouse suspicion.

Last fall General Gage sent out several hundred soldiers to build fortifications around

Boston Neck. Four large cannon are mounted there. And British guards at the Town Gate have become very cautious of late. Few townsmen are permitted to cross the Neck.

Once in Charlestown, Revere will borrow a horse from his friend Colonel William Conant. Conant, who belongs to the Sons of Liberty, is always eager to do anything he can to aid the patriots' cause.

Now Revere strides along the waterfront, passing the ropewalks where workmen once made cordage for the rigging of ships. He hastens by the foundries that melted down bog iron for anchors and chains. There's no longer the pungent odor of burning ore, so familiar to a man who has spent a lifetime in a thriving port. King George's closing of the port of Boston has halted every seaside activity.

It is still dark when Paul Revere reaches the small North End cove where he has hidden his rowboat. He bought the boat several months ago from Joseph Bentley, owner of Bentley's Boatyard and a member of Revere's spy network. Just last week Bentley stopped by the silversmith's shop, volunteering to do anything he could for Mr. Revere.

Pushing the boat into the water, Revere glances cautiously over his shoulder. Half-crouching, he steps into the small craft and shoves off from shore. Under cover of darkness he rows quickly across the half mile of water.

When he arrives on the Charlestown shore, Revere beaches his boat behind a tall clump of marsh weeds. He walks quickly into town and knocks on Colonel Conant's door. The Colonel is not too surprised at his early-morning caller. He has already heard rumors that trouble is brewing in Boston.

Revere explains that Dr. Warren has asked him to ride to Lexington to warn Adams and Hancock. From there he will go on to Concord and alert the patriots that they must find new hiding places for their stockpile of supplies. He will probably be gone most of the day, Revere adds. Warren has suggested he make this a leisurely ride so that no one will become

suspicious of his mission. Take the horse in the stable, Conant tells him, and welcome!

Like Boston, Charlestown is almost entirely surrounded by water. The only way out of town is across a narrow strip of land known as Charlestown Neck. It is a desolate patch of ground, filled with scrub growth, salt marshes, and clay pits.

The first rays of the rising sun light the road as Paul Revere travels out across the Neck, heading toward Lexington. Once he leaves this barren stretch, the road winds over gentle hills and through rolling farmlands. It has been an unusually warm spring in this part of the country. Farmers started their plowing and sowing and planting several weeks ago. Already the grass has turned green. The trees are beginning to bud. And in a few sheltered spots there's a scattering of flowers peeping out. As he canters along, Revere takes note of the neat little farms sprinkled on either side of the winding road. These farmers are known to be loyal patriots—all of them ready to take up arms at a moment's notice once the call is given.

The village of Lexington is just beginning to stir when Paul Revere rides into town. To give the appearance of a casual Sunday excursion, he slows the horse to a walk. The two amble past the barnlike meetinghouse in the center of Lexington Common. The common is an acre tract of land that was purchased more than sixty years ago to be "owned in common" by the residents of the village. It has long been the center of life for the people. There's a schoolhouse on the green, too, and a small belfry, which houses the town bell.

On the opposite side of the road is Buckman Tavern, where travelers often spend the night. At the far end of the common the road divides, one branch leading to Concord and the other to Bedford. Revere pulls on the reins, and the horse turns to the right, down the Bedford road.

About a quarter of a mile farther along, on the west side of the road, the parsonage comes

into view. It is here that John Hancock and
Sam Adams are staying as the guests of the
Reverend and Mrs. Jonas Clark. The Reverend Mr. Clark has been a patriot leader among
the people of Lexington ever since the move
toward independence began. And since Mrs.
Clark is John Hancock's cousin, their home
seemed a likely place for both men to stay in
safety for a few days before going on to Philadelphia and the Second Continental Congress.

Adams and Hancock are pleased to see Revere and eager to learn the news from Boston.
Things look grim, the rider explains. The
British are plotting something, although no
one knows where they will make their move—
or how soon. Dr. Warren has been watching
everything. His greatest fear now is that the
enemy are about to try to take Mr. Hancock
and Mr. Adams as prisoners.

Please be ready to leave Lexington at a
moment's notice, the rider urges, and be on
the alert for further messages. Revere himself
will try to get back with a warning once the

British plans are known. However, British patrols are everywhere. He may not be able to reach the Reverend Mr. Clark's home again.

His message delivered, Revere hurries out to his waiting horse. Hancock and Adams would have liked to hear more about what the enemy is doing in Boston. But the messenger is anxious to be on his way. Since there is a strong suspicion that the British have discovered the patriots' military stores in Concord, there is no time to lose.

Revere returns to Lexington Common and takes the road to the left, trotting along at an easy pace as he heads toward Concord. To give the appearance of a man taking a casual Sunday ride is not difficult on such a day as this. The sun is bright, the weather pleasantly warm for April. He hails several farmers along the way, stopping a few moments with each for a friendly chat. Should British spies be hidden in the nearby woods, they would never suspect that Paul Revere is a rider with important news to deliver.

Cantering into Concord, Revere goes directly to the home of Colonel James Barrett. For months now the patriots under Barrett's direction have been stockpiling supplies at the Town House. There are barrels of gunpowder, muskets, and cannon, as well as spades, axes, boxes of candles, salt, tents, medicine chests, and hogsheads of flour. Their hope was to gather all the necessary equipment for an army of fifteen thousand men.

Revere introduces himself to the colonel and explains his mission. Colonel Barrett understands the urgency of the message and promises that the precious supplies will be moved at once.

Before Revere leaves the village, he sees scores of men hurrying toward the Town House. Barrett has directed that guns, ammunition, and food are to be concealed in farm wagons and ox carts filled with straw. Everything will be hauled away and secretly hidden in the neighboring towns of Bedford, Canton, Acton, and Lancaster. If the British should march on Concord, they will find nothing.

During the return trip, Revere reviews the day's events. He has warned Adams and Hancock that possibly the British are soon to march. He has seen that the Concord patriots are moving their supplies to new hiding places. But once it is known when the British plan to attack, how can word be spread? This is a troublesome thought. He must find a way.

Back in Charlestown, Paul Revere returns the horse to Colonel Conant. As the two friends stand chatting in the colonel's front yard, Revere glances across the river at Boston.

Looming up above Copp's Hill, through the deepening dusk, the lofty steeple of Christ Church catches his eye. The steeple is by far the highest point in the town and clearly visible from the Charlestown shore. Why hasn't he thought of this before? The belfry window faces east toward Charlestown. It is the logical place from which to send a signal.

Excitedly Revere explains his plan to Conant. It is possible, he says, that once the British begin to move he may not be able to leave Boston. Yet Hancock and Adams must be warned. The minutemen must be alerted and the countryside aroused to the danger. If a lantern was flashed as a signal from the steeple of Christ Church, Conant could dispatch messengers at once.

But wait. The patriots will need to know how the enemy troops are moving out of Boston, whether by land or water. One light, Revere tells the colonel, will mean that they are marching by land, across Boston Neck through Roxbury and Brookline. Two lights are the signal that they are moving by water across the Charles River to Cambridge.

Keep a close watch on the steeple, Revere urges. The warning may flash at any time. It will have to be brief. They can't take a chance that the enemy will see it. And will the colonel please also have a horse ready? Revere is hoping to be able to row across the Charles River and take the message himself.

Conant reassures his friend that the Charlestown patriots will stand guard, keeping a constant lookout. As the two men part, the colonel repeats the signal: one if by land, two if by water.

Rowing back to the Boston shore, Revere goes over the details of his signal system. There's something else he must arrange. Someone will have to hang the signal lantern —or lanterns—in Christ Church steeple. Why not Robert Newman?

Twenty-three-year-old Newman is the caretaker of Christ Church. He lives nearby and knows the building well. What is more, he is very dependable, a faithful member of the Sons of Liberty.

After the boat has been once more safely hidden in the North End cove, Revere hustles over to Salem Street to see the caretaker. Young Newman is pleased to have a part in the plan. He will light the signal—just let him know when.

Now Paul Revere walks slowly back through the dark streets to his little house on North Square. He is elated with the success of today's mission. But the future appears grim. Should the British troops clash with the min-utemen at Lexington or Concord, it could mean war!

5

A KNOCK
AT THE DOOR

All day Monday, April seventeenth, a strange stillness hangs over Boston. The sky is a leaden gray with a threat of rain in the air. Members of Paul Revere's spy network patrol the streets, watching, waiting.

Over at Province House on Marlborough Street there is an unusual stir of activity. General Gage chose this square brick house for his headquarters when he arrived last summer. Some say he particularly liked the British lion and unicorn that are carved above the entrance. Today British officers are rushing in and out of the house in greater numbers than ever before. This is noted by the spy patrol

49

and duly reported to Paul Revere. No one, however, can put his finger on anything more specific.

By Tuesday the tensions are mounting steadily throughout the town. In his silver-smith shop on Fish Street, Revere and his son Paul sort out the orders that have been piling up these last few weeks. There are earrings to be repaired, shoe buckles to mend, several false teeth to be made. Revere finds it hard to concentrate on the work, although he is careful to hide his anxiety from his son.

Early in the afternoon John Ballard, a groom from the stable in Milk Street, brings the first specific news. He whispers to Revere that he has been acting like a British sympathizer so he can ask more questions. A groom from the Province House stable has just told him about a conversation he overheard while saddling the horses for a group of British officers.

The officers, who were joking about their disguise, were wearing long cloaks to hide

their swords. They are to tell everyone that they are going to Cambridge for a dinner party. But this is only a pretense. They have been ordered to ride out over Boston Neck and fan out through the countryside. If any-one asks what they are doing, they will say they are looking for deserters from the British army. Their real purpose, however, is to cap-ture any patriot messengers who may try to ride to Lexington or Concord.

This is important information. Revere is grateful to the young groom and thanks him for being so watchful. Every detail is useful in fitting together the puzzle of enemy plans.

Mrs. John Stedman from Winter Street is an afternoon caller at the silversmith's shop. She has some candelabra to be repaired. But her real purpose in coming, she confides, is to re-port a message she overheard an hour ago. Her serving-girl is the wife of a British soldier. One of the redcoats stopped at the Stedman home and told the girl that her husband, Gibson, must report to the lower part of Boston Common by eight o'clock tonight. He is to bring "a day's provisions and thirty-six rounds of ammunition."

Later in the afternoon gunsmith Jasper in Hatter's Square passes along word that a British sergeant-major told him the light infantry and grenadier units are being rounded up and ordered to report for duty. Another patriot saw a light infantry officer in full battle dress trying to buy something in one of the shops.

Rumors . . . rumors . . . rumors. Nothing definite yet. No word about what move the British plan.

As dusk falls, the silversmith decides not to return home for his evening meal. He will wait in the shop for some word from Dr. Warren. He must get a warning to Robert Newman though.

Revere turns to his son. Will Paul take a message to the caretaker of Christ Church? Tell Newman that tonight will probably be the night. That's message enough. Newman will understand. And be careful, Revere cautions his son. There are British officers quartered in the Newman household. They must not see a messenger come or go.

After young Paul leaves, the silversmith gazes out the window toward the harbor. The great hulk of a British man-of-war is moving silently through the water. The armed ship is probably being stationed there to stop any patriot who might try to get across the river to Charlestown.

Revere lights a brace of candles and seats himself on the bench beside his worktable. He fingers the tools aimlessly. Every muscle in his body is tense with anticipation. Surely some sort of word will soon come.

Shortly before ten the silversmith hears a faint sound. Is it a knock—or only the wind against the windowpanes? He glances apprehensively toward the door.

Again there's a light tap. Could this be a messenger? He crosses the room and opens the door a crack. Half-hidden in the shadows is a leather-aproned apprentice. The young man whispers only two words: "Dr. Warren."

The silversmith nods, and the messenger quickly disappears. This is the word Revere has been waiting for. Dr. Warren must know something definite.

The silversmith puts out the candles, locks his shop door, and sets off for Hanover Street. The stars are out, but there is a wind blowing in from the bay. Revere shivers as he strides through the deserted streets. The shutters are closed on nearly every house. If there's to be trouble tonight, most people are staying inside.

When Revere reaches Dr. Warren's house, the butler leads him directly back to the surgery where the doctor is pacing the floor. Warren has just learned that General Gage is to send more than a thousand troops to Concord. They will board waiting boats at the foot of the Common and be rowed across the river to Cambridge. From there the enemy will march on Lexington and Concord.

At the moment the doctor's greatest fear is

for the safety of Hancock and Adams. William Dawes of Ann Street was here when word came that the British are marching. Does Revere by any chance know Billy Dawes?

The silversmith doesn't know him well, he says. But Dawes is a member of the Sons of Liberty and must be quite an actor. There have been several stories about his pretending to be a drunken farmer and slipping through the guards at the town gate.

Billy Dawes volunteered to leave at once to take the message to Hancock and Adams, the doctor tells Revere. He will ride out across Boston Neck if he is able to get through the town gate. He hopes to bribe the guards, although there is no assurance his plan will work. If he is successful, he will take the road through Roxbury and Cambridge to Lexington.

Riding across Boston Neck isn't the only way to spread the alarm, Revere counters. He tells the doctor about the plan he concocted with Conant last Sunday. Because Christ

Church is plainly visible from the Charles-town shore, he has arranged a signal system. The caretaker, Robert Newman, will handle the signals. If the British are moving out by land, he will hang one lantern. If they go by water, there will be two lanterns.

Colonel Conant has promised to be watching for the signal. The moment the lights appear, he will dispatch a messenger to Lexington. Conant will have a horse ready for Revere, too. The silversmith is determined to try to cross the river by rowboat and take the message personally to Hancock and Adams.

Does Revere realize how dangerous such a plan has become? the doctor asks. The British frigate *Somerset* was moved into the mouth of the Charles River only a few hours ago. There will be sentinels on deck, keeping a constant watch, waiting to fire on anything that arouses their suspicion. Trying to cross the river in a small skiff might mean death.

Revere knows all this—but he's willing to take the risk. Now he must hurry over to

Salem Street and alert young Newman to hang two signal lights in the belfry.

Dr. Warren grasps the hand of his friend and wishes him Godspeed as Paul Revere hurries toward the front door.

6

TWO LANTERNS
TO HANG

After leaving Dr. Warren's house, Paul Revere meets a number of soldiers hurrying toward the Common, dressed in full battle gear. He lowers his head quickly and looks the other way so that the soldiers will not recognize him. This is no time to be stopped by the British.

Revere crosses Union Street and walks up toward Christ Church. He is startled by a tall figure stepping out of the shadows just ahead. Revere recognizes Robert Newman, the very man he is seeking.

Newman explains that his mother's house is full of British officers tonight. They are playing cards in the parlor. The young caretaker feared it might be awkward for Mr. Revere to call at the front door. Suppose he should be seen by one of the officers? Or what if their conversation were overheard?

About nine o'clock, therefore, Newman announced that he was going to bed and went upstairs to his room. From there he climbed out through the second-floor window, slipped across a shed roof, and dropped to the ground. He could still hear the loud talk and laughter of the officers as he stole out of the yard, so he is sure no one is aware of his escape.

John Pulling, a vestryman of Christ Church, is to be waiting for them at the front door, Newman continues. Pulling has the keys and will let Newman into the church. He has also promised to stand guard at the entrance while the caretaker climbs to the steeple.

The two friends stride along silently until they reach the walk leading up to the church. As they turn in, a third man steps out from behind a clump of bushes. Robert Newman introduces the vestryman, and the two shake hands.

In hushed tones Paul Revere tells his companions that Dr. Warren has just had definite word the British are moving by boat to Cambridge. Revere himself is about to leave for Charlestown. He plans to row across the river, then ride to Lexington to warn Hancock and Adams that the redcoats are marching.

Pulling wonders why they must send a signal, if Revere is himself going to Charlestown.

He may never reach Charlestown, Revere explains. The British warship *Somerset* has moved into the harbor. Dr. Warren believes that guards on the ship will be watching every small craft, ready to shoot any patriot who may try to cross the river. If Revere fails to reach Charlestown, the colonel and his friends can dispatch other messengers.

Now does Newman have the lanterns ready?

They are hidden under the stairs in the belfry, the caretaker whispers. But which signal should he give?

Hang two lanterns in the belfry, Revere says. Then the people on the Charlestown shore will know the British are crossing by boat to Cambridge.

John Pulling questions whether the lights can actually be seen so far away. Revere explains that as a boy he was a bell ringer for Christ Church. Many times from the tower he looked over to the Charlestown shore. What's more, he knows the exact spot in Charlestown where the steeple can be seen. He pointed it out to Colonel Conant only last Sunday. The colonel has promised to keep a lookout there.

How long does Mr. Revere want the lanterns left in the steeple? Newman asks.

Revere says they should be left only a very short time—just long enough to alert the patriots in Charlestown. Great care must be taken, though. With the enemy ship *Somerset* now in the harbor, the guards could easily spot any unusual light.

Pulling suggests that perhaps Newman should light a lantern, once he is inside the church. The stairs leading up to the belfry are narrow. If he has to climb them in the dark, Newman may run the risk of a terrible fall.

Revere vetoes this suggestion abruptly. The lookout in Charlestown might see the single light and think the British are marching by land.

There's really no danger of falling, Revere assures Pulling. The silversmith knows every step in the tower. All Newman needs to do is to keep to the left of the stair. The opening where the bells hang is on the right side. It's not a bad climb, if you use your left hand to guide you along the wall.

Remember the signals, Paul Revere cautions Newman once more. Two lanterns—but hang them only for a few moments.

Newman nods and reminds Mr. Revere that he is taking a great risk in trying to cross the Charles River and ride to Lexington. Revere's face is grim with determination. There are many tonight who are risking their lives.

In parting, the silversmith suggests that

Newman hang the two lanterns well apart. The Charlestown lookout must know there are *two* signal lights. As John Pulling unlocks the church door, Revere strides off toward North Square.

Robert Newman, feeling his way through the darkness, locates the stairway to the belfry tower. The deep silence of the church is broken only by an occasional creak of the stairs, an eerie sound that echoes through the pitch-blackness. Once in the tower, the young man pulls out the lanterns from their hiding place.

Now for the long flight of stairs into the steeple. Carefully he creeps up, one by one, guiding his steps by holding his left hand against the wall, just as Mr. Revere has suggested.

There's the yawning cavity that holds the eight bells of Christ Church, the bells that people say have a royal peal. No danger of falling, though, as long as he stays well to the left. Up and up he climbs until he reaches the belfry platform. Glancing out the small window, Newman sees the outline of Charlestown across the river. Will Colonel Conant's lookout be watching?

With trembling fingers the young man lights the two lanterns and holds them far apart at the window. Mr. Revere said to keep them there for only a very short time.

As he blows out the candles, Robert Newman can only hope that the signals have been seen by the Charlestown patriots. He grasps both lanterns in his left hand and guides himself by the wall on the right as he descends.

A sound of voices outside the church startles the caretaker. Better not try to leave through the front door. He will climb out a window in the back of the church and slip home by way of Unity and Bennett streets. If he were seen coming out of the front entrance to Christ Church at this hour, he would certainly be subject to questioning. And tonight of all nights is no time for the British to become suspicious.

7

STEALING ACROSS
THE CHARLES

Over in North Square the redcoats are gathering quickly. There's a sharp clank of sabers as the men begin to line up in the Square— evidence enough that General Gage means business tonight.

Hurrying home, Paul Revere hears the muted shouts of British officers ordering their men into formation. As he reaches North Square, soldiers seem to be coming from every direction. Just a few steps ahead, Revere sees one of his neighbors being stopped. The guard detail has surrounded the man. They seem to be asking all sorts of questions. Perhaps the redcoats are looking for a silversmith who knows too much. Revere steps back into the shadows and turns down the alley. It will be safer to enter his house by way of the back door.

Rachel is waiting in the kitchen. By the dim light of a single candle, Revere notes that his wife's face is pale and taut with worry. Hastily he explains that he must leave for Lexington tonight to warn Hancock and Adams. He has come home only to put on heavy boots and pick up his woolen surtout. The night has turned chilly—he'll need a heavy coat before morning. There's not a moment to waste. North Square is filled with redcoats, armed and ready to march.

It is a difficult moment for both husband and wife. Rachel is trembling as Revere kisses her good-bye. It's possible they may never see each other again. But this is no time to lose courage. Wordlessly he turns and hurries out the back door.

As Revere sets off at a rapid pace, he feels something brush against his legs. It's his faithful brown spaniel. He orders the dog to go home, but the animal is not to be shaken off so easily. No matter. Perhaps a man walking with his pet will arouse less suspicion than a person hurrying through the dark streets alone.

Ducking in and out of alleys to avoid the redcoats, Revere heads for the North End cove where his boat is hidden. As he nears the hiding place, two men step forward from the shadows. Revere recognizes them as members of his spy ring—Josh Bentley and Tom Richardson.

Bentley whispers that Dr. Warren has sent word that he and Richardson are to row Mr. Revere across the Charles River. That way Revere can save all his energy for the dash to Lexington.

At the mention of the ride, the silversmith stops short. In his haste to leave home, he has forgotten to bring his spurs. He will be riding a strange horse. Speed will be essential. He must have the spurs. Yet to go back now through the heavily patrolled streets is unthinkable.

Then Revere sees his brown spaniel standing expectantly beside him, ears cocked and tail wagging. The spaniel has been so quiet the silversmith forgot all about him. Taking a slip of paper from his pocket, Revere scribbles a single word on it, "Spurs," and attaches the paper securely to his pet's collar. With a loving pat and a whispered command, he sends the dog home.

The three men now pull the boat from its hiding place. When Bentley slips an oar into the oarlock, there's a sharp clink. The men look at each other in horror. Noise such as this will attract attention to their boat before they are twenty yards offshore. Some way must be found to muffle the sound of the oars.

Richardson has an inspiration. His girl lives at the corner of North and North-Center streets. That's not far. He'll see what he can do.

Within a few minutes Richardson returns, grinning sheepishly. He reports that he stood under the girl's window and whistled their special signal. When she opened the window, he told her what was needed—something to muffle the oars. Without hesitation, she threw down her flannel petticoat. (Years later, Mr. Revere will tell his grandchildren that when they got the petticoat it was "still warm.")

While Richardson tears the petticoat into strips, Revere and Bentley wrap the flannel around tholepins and gunnels. They work feverishly, knowing that every second is important. As soon as the oars are muffled, the men shove the boat into the water.

Farther upstream Revere sights boatloads of British troops already crossing over to Cambridge. Out near Barton's Point is the British ship *Somerset,* the 64-gun frigate that was moved into the narrowest point in the river only hours ago. Its sole purpose is to discourage any patriot who is thinking of leaving Boston. The ship's huge bulk has cut off the shortest route to Charlestown. This means the small rowboat will have to move farther out to sea if the men are to escape detection. Even worse, a full moon is rising. It will soon be lighting up the river, the entire countryside. How can the sentries aboard the *Somerset* fail to see three men in a rowboat?

Hastily Bentley and Richardson take their places in the center of the boat, ready to man the oars. Revere is about to step into the stern when he hears the soft pad, pad of a dog's feet coming toward him. His spaniel pushes through the tall weeds, panting breathlessly, the spurs jangling at his collar.

Either the British patrol did not see the dog, or they were not quick enough to catch him. In either case Paul Revere is grateful to his fleet-footed pet. After unloosing the spurs, he pats the dog and again sends him home.

Now Revere seats himself in the stern, and the boat shoves off. Richardson and Bentley send the small craft through the water with sure, even strokes. Not a word is spoken. Revere is motionless, shoulders hunched, eyes fixed on the menacing guns of the warship.

As the boat reaches the middle of the river, Revere signals to the men to stop rowing. Even the telltale flash of wet oars may attract attention. The boat drifts seaward, and all three bend low, hardly daring to breathe. At any second there may be shouts of alarm, a roar of gunfire that will break the uneasy quiet of the river.

Once past the *Somerset,* Revere motions Bentley and Richardson to start rowing again.

Quietly they dip the oars into the water, pulling more swiftly as they ease the small skiff toward the eastern shoreline. Very shortly the boat grazes the stones of the beach. All three sigh with relief. They have made it. No shot was fired from the *Somerset*. They are still alive, something they hardly expected when they left Boston.

Murmuring his thanks, Revere leaps out of the boat and makes his way up the rocky beach. His night's mission has only begun. Now he must find Colonel Conant—and a horse to ride.

8

BRIEF STOP
IN CHARLESTOWN

All Charlestown seems to be slumbering as Paul Revere half walks, half runs through the darkened streets. The salty breeze blowing in from the sea has a chilling effect. Revere pulls his coat collar up around his face, as much for disguise as for protection against the wind. Better not to be recognized—just in case there are British soldiers somewhere about.

Rounding a corner, Revere sees the dim glow of candlelight in Conant's front parlor. He can distinguish the shadowy forms of several men in the room. Surely the patrol must have seen Robert Newman's lanterns from Christ Church steeple.

Revere's sharp rap on the door brings the colonel, who can scarcely believe his eyes. With the *Somerset*'s guns trained on the water, he never expected Paul Revere to make it across the Charles.

The messenger's first question is about the signal. Did they see the two lights? Has a messenger been sent out to alert the countryside?

The answer is yes to both questions, Colonel Conant says, leading Revere into the parlor. After hasty introductions, Conant explains that he has grave doubts as to whether his messenger has been able to get through to sound the alarm. In fact, he wonders if Revere himself can possibly reach Lexington. The county is crawling with British soldiers on patrol tonight.

Among the gentlemen gathered at Colonel Conant's house is Mr. Richard Devens, a member of the Committee of Safety and Supplies. Devens reports that he and Abraham Watson were attending a meeting of the committee over in Menotomy. They were riding home about sundown when they met ten British officers cantering along the Lexington road. Though the officers pretended they were out on a party, their long blue cloaks did not conceal the fact that they were armed.

The officers stopped Devens' chaise and asked for directions to Clark's Tavern. Devens' answer was vague, since he realized the officers must be looking for Jonas Clark's parsonage, possibly to arrest Hancock and Adams. No doubt they had been told to go to "Clark's," and they assumed it was a tavern rather than a private home.

Alarmed by the idea that the rebel leaders might be captured, Devens turned his chaise around as soon as the officers were out of sight. He and Watson cut across several fields to get back to Menotomy ahead of the British. From there he sent a messenger to Lexington to warn Hancock and Adams. But there is no certainty that his man was able to get past the network of British patrols, now flung like a gigantic spider web across the countryside.

The knowledge that there are many enemy soldiers out tonight on the Middlesex County roads does not stop Paul Revere. He has no gun—and for a good reason. Not being armed will make him appear more innocent. Should a patrol attempt to capture him, he will try to outwit or outride them. There are back roads, too, and shortcuts through fields of which the British are unaware. Revere has but one mission tonight—he must reach Lexington to warn the patriot leaders. But he will need a swift horse to slip through the network.

Colonel Conant leads Revere outside. The horse is ready, all saddled and bridled. It's a Yankee-bred animal, slender and nervous. Deacon John Larkin, one of Charlestown's wealthiest citizens, has lent the best horse in his stable for Mr. Revere's ride, Conant explains.

With one swift glance, Revere measures the courage and stamina of his future companion. Compared to the heavy British mounts, this horse is small in size. But that is an advantage. He can probably outdistance any pursuer. Tonight Revere's life and the lives of many other patriots may depend on the fleetness of this handsome little beast.

Quickly the new master adjusts the stirrups to the proper length. Next, the bit. Then Revere slips a forefinger under the saddle to check the snugness of the girths. They should be firm but not tight. As he performs these preliminaries, Revere strokes the horse, talking gently in reassuring tones. These two have a long night ahead. He wants to make sure they are friends.

Now the rider swings into the saddle and asks the time. It's almost eleven o'clock, Conant says.

Revere advises the colonel that he will ride out across Charlestown Neck, then through Somerville to Cambridge. From there he will go on to Lexington. That is the shortest way. He'll be able to make the best time taking this route.

The Ride of
Paul Revere
April 18-19, 1775

Conant raises his hand in a gesture of silent farewell as Paul Revere gallops off. At this moment much depends on the patriot rider. Will he get through to Lexington? Or will there be a British patrol hidden somewhere in the shadows ready to seize him?

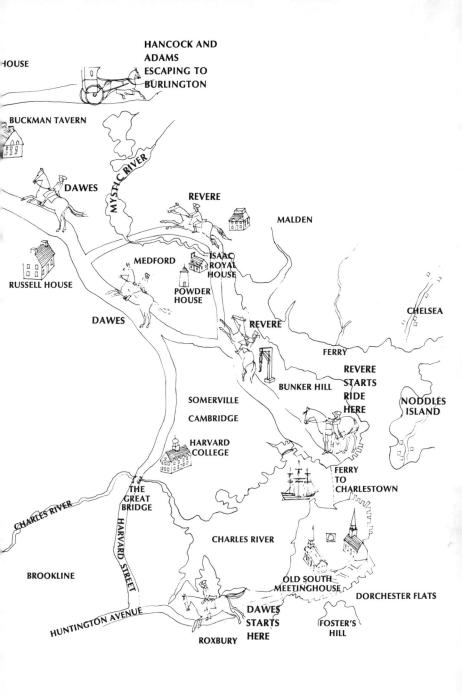

HANCOCK AND
ADAMS
ESCAPING TO
BURLINGTON

HOUSE

BUCKMAN TAVERN

DAWES

MYSTIC RIVER

REVERE

MALDEN

MEDFORD

ISAAC
ROYAL
HOUSE

RUSSELL HOUSE

POWDER
HOUSE

CHELSEA

DAWES

REVERE

FERRY

BUNKER HILL

REVERE
STARTS
RIDE
HERE

NODDLES
ISLAND

SOMERVILLE

CAMBRIDGE

HARVARD
COLLEGE

FERRY
TO
CHARLESTOWN

CHARLES RIVER

THE
GREAT
BRIDGE

HARVARD STREET

CHARLES RIVER

BROOKLINE

OLD SOUTH
MEETINGHOUSE

DORCHESTER FLATS

HUNTINGTON AVENUE

DAWES
STARTS
HERE

FOSTER'S
HILL

ROXBURY

9

NEAR-CAPTURE

Tonight Charlestown Neck seems more desolate than ever. As Paul Revere rides briskly along, the newly risen moon shines over the lonely countryside. The thud of hoofbeats is the only sound, one that seems to echo and re-echo across the moors.

Revere paces his horse carefully. He would like to gallop along at full speed. But Devens has warned that a British patrol may suddenly appear. If this happens, the little native mount must be ready for that extra spurt of speed. This will be essential if the rider is to escape his pursuers.

Midway across the Neck, the road forks. Revere takes the branch to the left. It is sandy, rutted, and narrow, but it leads directly into Cambridge. The ride to Lexington will be several miles shorter along this route. Just last Sunday he took this same road. He is thoroughly familiar with every twist and turn. He knows where the hazardous clay pits are located, where there are clusters of trees that might hide potential enemies.

Only a few miles out of Charlestown, Revere glimpses a rusty iron cage dangling from a tree along the roadside. The cage holds the bleached skeleton of a slave, Mark, who was hanged here twenty years ago by his master from whom he had tried to escape. This is a grim reminder of the dangers of defying authority. If the patriot leaders are captured, they will undoubtedly be sent to London and hanged for treason. Revere looks away, shuddering, and gallops straight ahead.

Whenever he approaches a turn in the road, the rider pulls on the reins and peers sharply around, before digging his spurs into the horse's flanks and galloping on. Are there redcoats lurking in some hidden spot? Every thicket of trees, each patch of shadows, is an ominous threat. A shot may ring out at any moment.

Revere's keen eyes search the countryside, shifting back and forth. He must be alert for any unusual sight or sound. If he is to elude the British and get through to Lexington, he must see the enemy first. He must be ready with a plan of escape.

Now he is almost across the Neck. Only one more group of trees lies ahead. Then suddenly he sees it—a gleam of light that could only be reflected from a highly polished pistol holster. He reins his horse to an abrupt stop as two British officers lunge out from the shadows. One plunges straight toward Paul Revere as the other gallops up the road. Revere realizes that the second officer will be able to trap him if the first officer fails to capture him.

In the split second that follows, Revere's quick mind devises a plan. He'll dash directly cross-country, and if he can shake off his pursuers, take the alternate road. He whirls his horse sharply to the right and digs in the spurs, clearing the low roadside wall in a flying leap.

For a moment the first British officer is taken aback. He hardly expected Revere to take off through an open wasteland. But he spurs his heavy military charger and is off in pursuit of the patriot rider.

Galloping at top speed, Revere leans low over the horse's neck, turning his head just enough to make sure the British officer is not gaining on him. There are boulders to side-step, clumps of bayberry thicket to avoid. Fortunately, Deacon Larkin's native-bred animal is more fleet-footed than the British charger. Indeed, the officer is dropping back slightly.

There's a clay pond straight ahead. Tall grass hides its slippery banks. Revere swings quickly to one side and turns just in time to avoid the treacherous hole. But an instant later he hears the frantic thud of sliding hoofs. The British officer was not aware of the clay pond.

Now his charger is floundering in the sticky mire.

Having successfully shaken off his would-be captor, Paul Revere speeds across the waste-land until he reaches the road that parallels the Mystic River. Now he can give his horse full rein. Before long the sleeping village of Medford comes into sight. On the spur of the moment he decides to alarm the inhabitants of this little ship-building town. The more people who know the British are coming, the better the defense will be. His horse thunders across the plank bridge spanning the Mystic. Down the village street he gallops until he reaches the home of Captain Isaac Hall of Medford's minutemen.

There is no time to dismount and knock on the door. Revere leans out of his saddle and hammers on the siding with his whip handle.

An upstairs window flies up.

"The British regulars are out, bound for Concord!" shouts the rider.

The captain springs to action. Others, too, have heard the messenger's alarm. Before Revere leaves the village, a small lad is racing to ring the church bell. Older boys, still not old enough to shoulder a musket, run for their horses. They will ride through Middlesex County to spread the word along the back roads. An old man steps out with his drum, his sticks beating the alarm.

Galloping west out of Medford, Revere recrosses the Mystic River and rides on to Arlington Center. There he turns northwest at Cooper Tavern and picks up the road to Lexington. This is the road he had intended to take before the British patrol forced him to detour.

At every farmhouse along the way Revere shouts out his alarm. In some instances the sleeping inhabitants are awakened by the sound of flying hoofs. If a lamp appears in the window, Revere does not stop to rein up, merely shouting as he passes, "The British regulars are coming. Spread the alarm!"

If the farmer is sleeping soundly, Revere rides up to the door and pounds loudly, calling out: "The regulars are coming! To arms, to arms!"

All over the countryside people are awakening to the coming danger. Beacon fires are lighted. Muskets are shot off as warning signals. Church bells clang; drums beat. Minutemen run from their homes, muskets in hand and powder horns slung over their shoulders.

They are beginning to form up in companies as they have been trained to do.

Paul Revere's alarm spreads rapidly. The rider is exhilarated by the noise, the action that his alarm has aroused. But most of all, Revere knows he must get the warning to Hancock and Adams. Through the bright moonlight he speeds on toward Lexington.

10

MISSION COMPLETED

Late that afternoon Solomon Brown, a young Lexington minuteman, had been returning from Boston. Along the road he encountered several British officers who were trying to give the appearance of taking a leisurely ride. Underneath the officers' long blue cloaks, however, the observant Brown noted the men were wearing side arms—something General Gage had forbidden when officers rode into the countryside for pleasure. This seemed suspicious to the young minuteman. He must report it at once.

The Britishers paid little attention to Solomon Brown as he spurred his horse and raced past them, heading for Lexington. Once in town he reined up at Munroe's Tavern and hurried inside to find the innkeeper, William Munroe, who is orderly sergeant of the Lexington minutemen. Excitedly Brown gave the details of what he had seen, adding that the officers acted as if "they did not care to reach there until the shades of evening had set in."

Sergeant Munroe jumped to the conclusion that these British officers were on their way to arrest Reverend Jonas Clark's distinguished guests—John Hancock and Sam Adams. Action must be taken at once. Munroe ordered an armed guard of eight men including himself to surround the Reverend Mr. Clark's home out on the Bedford road.

Around nine o'clock the British officers rode through Lexington and disappeared down the Concord road. The news spread rapidly, and the minutemen held a quick conference with the Reverend Jonas Clark. It was decided that the officers should be followed in case they tried to double back to Lexington. Two other young minutemen, Elijah Sanderson and Jonathan Loring, were assigned the task of trailing the Britishers with Solomon Brown. Brown said he would be glad to go, but he needed a fresh horse. The Reverend Mr. Clark offered his mount, which Brown accepted gratefully.

The three minutemen, willing but inexperienced in the ways of spying, rode off to trail the officers. At about ten o'clock they had the misfortune to ride directly into a trap which the Britishers had set for them in Lincoln, only a few miles from Lexington.

Sometime later, Elijah Sanderson recounted that "one rode up and seized my bridle and another my arm, and one put his pistol to my breast, and told me if I resisted, I was a dead man . . . . He ordered me to get off my horse. Several of them dismounted and led us into a field." For the next few hours the minutemen were questioned in detail, particularly about where Hancock and Adams could be found.

Now it is nearly midnight.

Paul Revere, galloping into Lexington, is unaware, of course, that the three young minutemen have been captured. All is silent in the sleeping village. He spurs his horse even faster, no longer fearing the sudden appearance of a British patrol. Past the meeting-house he speeds, past Buckman Tavern, and out the Bedford road.

As Revere approaches the rambling gabled dwelling of the Reverend Jonas Clark, he is startled to see the detail of patriot guards posted around the house. Quickly he dismounts and demands to be admitted.

Sergeant Munroe explains in a low voice that the ladies and gentlemen have retired and have asked "not to be disturbed by any noise."

"Noise!" explodes Revere. "You'll have noise enough before long. The British regulars are out."

The rider brushes past the guard and knocks loudly on the front door.

One of the upstairs windows flies up, and the massive head of the Reverend Mr. Clark appears. He does not recognize Paul Revere in the dark and says he will not admit any stranger at this time of night.

In his first-floor bedroom John Hancock, who is not yet asleep, recognizes the voice of his friend, Revere. "Come in, Revere," he calls out. "We're not afraid of you!"

Still clad in nightshirts, Hancock and Adams usher the messenger into the Clarks' front parlour. Quickly Revere reports that Dr. Warren has sent him with a warning. The patriot leaders must leave at once. "More than a thousand light troops" are on the way. Revere himself has seen them on the Charles River going toward Cambridge tonight as he stole across in his rowboat to Charlestown.

Dr. Warren is certain the British will march to Lexington to capture the rebel leaders and then go on to Concord to seize the ammunition and supplies. He sent Revere through Charlestown. Billy Dawes was to ride out by land with the same message. Has he arrived yet?

No, Adams replies. This is the first news they have had that a large number of British soldiers are on their way to Lexington. They must make preparations to leave at once. Adams hurries out to Sergeant Munroe to ask that the guard detail help spread the alarm.

Meanwhile, John Hancock is calling for his sword and gun. He is determined to join the Lexington minutemen and fight the British. Coming back into the room, Sam Adams has difficulty in calming his friend. Patiently he argues that both men have been elected as delegates to the Second Continental Congress in Philadelphia. They will be leaving in a few days. They must not do anything so foolhardy now as to make themselves open targets for the British.

At this moment there is a clatter of hoofs outside. It is Billy Dawes arriving from Boston. He reports that he bribed the sentries at the gate on Boston Neck and escaped through

Roxbury. His ride has been uneventful—
after he left Boston, not a British soldier in
sight.

Mrs. Clark suggests that the two messengers
must be hungry, and she bustles about the
kitchen getting them some supper. While Revere and Dawes consume the food, they dis-
cuss their next move. True, their mission is
completed. They have warned the rebel leaders, as Dr. Warren had asked them to do. But
what about Concord?

Even though Revere had warned Colonel
Barrett in Concord just two days ago to start
hiding their supplies, the minutemen still
must be alerted. The two messengers decide
to ride the five miles farther to Concord. They
will alarm the farmers along the way. The
more people who know that the British are
coming, the better prepared the colonists will
be.

The Reverend Mr. Clark tells Revere and
Dawes about the officers who rode through
Lexington earlier this evening, adding that

he dispatched three minutemen to trail them. Nothing further has been heard from them. The minister has no idea what has happened.

After thanking Mrs. Clark for her hospitality, the messengers hurry out to mount their waiting horses. Only five more miles to Concord. Possibly they can get there in time!

I I

"HALT!"

It is nearly one o'clock in the morning when Paul Revere and William Dawes leave the Reverend Mr. Clark's parsonage. The food refreshed the messengers, and the horses are now rested. As the two men ride through Lexington, they hear the continuous clang of the meetinghouse bell. There are lighted candles in almost every house. People are stirring now that they have heard the alarm.

Just beyond the Lexington green the two men hear the clip-clop of horses' hoofs coming up behind them. They rein in and wait for the rider. He may be a British soldier.

The horseman, recognizing Paul Revere,

introduces himself as Dr. Samuel Prescott of
Concord, a member of the Sons of Liberty.
He has been calling on Miss Lydia Mulliken,
he explains. Her brother, Nathaniel, is one
of the Lexington minutemen and was alerted
a few minutes ago about the British march.
Dr. Prescott is on his way home, hoping to
arouse Concord citizens before the troops
reach his town.

The physician would like to join Revere
and Dawes. He wants to help spread the alarm
on the way to Concord. He knows every house-
holder along the way. Certainly the farmers
will "give more credit" to his words, he says,
than they would to an alarm shouted out by
complete strangers.

Before Paul Revere accepts Dr. Prescott's
offer, he warns him that they may be captured
by a British patrol. Armed soldiers are known
to have spread through the countryside. They
may be stopped at any time.

But Prescott is quite ready to take the risk.
The men gallop three abreast along the road.

Moonlight silvers the rolling hills and casts intricate patterns under the trees along the roadside. The riders peer through the shadows at anything that seems to be moving. Each man is tense, alert for a possible ambush.

About three miles out of Lexington, Prescott and Dawes stop at a farmhouse to awaken the owner while Paul Revere rides on. Suddenly, just ahead in the shadows, he sees two mounted British soldiers riding toward him.

"Come up! There are two of them," Revere shouts to Prescott and Dawes. Before his friends can join him, two more soldiers ride out from the bushes just behind Revere. He is trapped!

Sizing up the situation, Billy Dawes whirls his horse around and gallops off toward a deserted farmhouse to escape the enemy. The horse stumbles, tossing Dawes off as he goes down. But at least Dawes is not caught in the trap, and he starts back in the direction of Lexington on foot.

Meanwhile, Sam Prescott decides to try to

bluff his way out. After all, he is a physician and has the privilege of riding wherever he pleases. Just as he reaches Revere's side, a soldier shouts, "Halt! If you go an inch further, you're a dead man!" Prescott uses the butt end of his whip, trying to force a path. But the officers, with pistols drawn, threaten to blow out the brains of the first man who attempts to move.

Now surrounded by the enemy, Revere and Prescott are told to turn into a small pasture beside the road. The four British officers are riding closely behind their captives when suddenly Prescott digs his heels into his horse's flanks.

Prescott veers sharply to the left. Horse and rider fly over a low stone wall and take off pell-mell through the rough terrain. Revere turns to the right and makes for a small woods up ahead, hoping to get away from his captors. Just as he reaches the thicket, six more British officers rush out, seize his bridle, and order him to dismount.

When Revere gets off his horse, the officer in command rides up and begins to question him. Where does he come from? What time did he leave? Revere answers that he is from Boston and that he left at ten o'clock.

The officer, whom Paul Revere will later describe as "much of a gentleman," says, "Sir, may I crave your name?"

"My name is Revere."

"What?" shouts the commander in surprise. "Paul Revere?"

"Yes," answers Revere quietly. Knowing that his midnight alarm is now spreading rapidly, he adds defiantly, "But you will miss your aim."

The officer tells him that they are only out tonight to look for deserters from the British army.

"I know better," Revere contradicts him. "I know what you are after, but I have alarmed the country all the way along."

The startled commander rides up the road to confer with the officers who first stopped

Revere, moments before. Within minutes they all approach Revere at a full gallop.

Major Edward Mitchell of the Fifth Regiment claps his pistol to Revere's head. "If you do not tell the truth," he roars, "I'll blow your brains out."

The questioning begins again, and Revere gives "much the same answers" as before. Mitchell, after searching him for arms, orders the prisoner to remount his horse.

Revere reaches for the reins, but Major Mitchell grabs them out of his hands. "Good sir," says Mitchell, "you are not to ride with reins, I assure you," and he hands the reins to the British sergeant on Revere's right.

As the group moves off toward the Lexington-Concord road, they are joined by more British officers who have four prisoners with them. Revere rightly suspects that three of the prisoners are the young minutemen whom the Reverend Jonas Clark dispatched to follow the British several hours ago. So they, too, have been trapped!

The fourth prisoner is a one-armed peddler who was merely getting an early start for Concord and wandered innocently into the enemy network.

Major Mitchell turns toward Revere, saying, "We are now going toward your friends, and if you attempt to run or we are insulted, we will blow your brains out."

The patriot retorts that the major may do as he pleases.

When the British officers and their prisoners are about half a mile from the Lexington meetinghouse, the sound of rifle fire splits the air.

What is that, the major wants to know.

"It's to alarm the countryside," Paul Revere replies defiantly.

Thinking that the Britishers might be caught in a trap, the major issues an order. The girths and bridles must be cut on the horses belonging to Sanderson, Loring, Solomon Brown, and the peddler, so their animals cannot be ridden. The men are told to return home on foot, and their horses are driven into a nearby field.

Revere has hopes that he, too, will be set free. But the British close in around him, and they once more ride on. They travel only a short distance before a second shot rings out —and then a third.

The major begins to wonder if, after all, their prisoner may not have told him the truth. Perhaps Lexington Common is swarming with minutemen ready to fire on the redcoats. If the patrol should really be in danger, they would have a far better chance to escape without the burden of a prisoner. They must get word to the approaching British troops.

Acting on impulse, the major holds up his hand and halts the patrol. Revere is ordered to dismount. He wonders if this is the moment the enemy has chosen to put a bullet through his back.

Major Mitchell turns to the sergeant and asks him if his horse is tired. (Revere notes that the redcoat is riding a small horse, much

smaller than the usual heavy chargers of the British army.) When the sergeant replies that his horse is very tired, Mitchell barks out an order that the sergeant is to take Revere's horse and make use of it "for the night." Then turning to Revere, the major inquires how far it is to Cambridge and if there is another road.

Before Revere has finished answering, the Britishers are digging their spurs into the flanks of their mounts and galloping up the dusty road. Now the patriot is left alone, dazed by the events of the last few minutes. Deacon Larkin's trusty little mare is gone, probably forever. But Paul Revere is no longer a captive of the British army.

12

"IF THEY MEAN TO HAVE A WAR"

As the dust settles after the departing British, Paul Revere feels his knees trembling with relief. He is free at last! The past hour has been a frightening one—not knowing whether he will be shot on the spot or sent to London and hanged as a traitor.

Now he is no longer a prisoner of the British. As the tautness of his body begins to relax, Revere reminds himself that he must still be alert for further trouble. He decides not to walk along the roadside. There may be other patrols waiting to trap him. He doesn't want to chance being captured again.

Instead Paul Revere cuts across the adjoining pasture. The spurs on his boots make walking difficult. He stoops over and detaches them, tucking them into his coat pocket. As he does so, he is reminded of the faithful pet who trotted back to North Square and returned with the needed spurs just as he was ready to shove off for Charlestown. Was it only five hours ago? It seems more like five days.

Paul Revere is not familiar with the outskirts of Lexington, but when he stumbles over some gravestones, he is certain that the Reverend Mr. Clark's house cannot be far. He tramps through the field behind the Harrington house, north of the Common, and within a few minutes sees the outline of the rambling frame parsonage through the darkness.

There's a light glowing in every room. Evidently the guests have not yet departed. Drawing nearer, Revere can hear John Hancock still arguing that he must go out and fight the oncoming troops himself. Adams is saying that active fighting is not their business. The two patriot leaders belong to the government. They must get to Philadelphia for the opening session of the Continental Congress. Only then can they persuade the other colonies to join in this fight for freedom. They must leave actual combat to the men who are trained for it.

Paul Revere's appearance is a surprise to the entire household. Everyone is up and dressed now. They have been joined by John Lowell, Mr. Hancock's secretary, who is staying at Buckman Tavern. Lowell had heard the commotion on the Common and hurried over to see if he could assist his employer.

Hancock and Adams are eager to know what has happened to Revere. The messenger relates how he was captured by the British patrol and questioned for more than an hour. Everyone agrees that the British must mean business. John Hancock decides that perhaps he should leave with Sam Adams after all.

The Reverend Mr. Clark offers them his carriage for the escape. He suggests that the two patriot leaders ride over to the village of Woburn. That should prove a safe enough hideout for the next few days.

While the carriage is being brought around, the guests complete their packing. Trunks are stowed away, and at exactly four twenty, Hancock, Adams, and the secretary, John Lowell, climb into the carriage. Hancock suggests that Paul Revere accompany them, also. The patriot messenger is pleased with the invitation and squeezes in beside Lowell.

Sergeant Munroe leads the party out to the north of Lexington and starts them on the road to Woburn. They jog along in silence for almost two miles. Then John Hancock suddenly orders the carriage to stop. He has just had a horrifying thought. The trunk with all his important papers has been left in Lowell's room at Buckman Tavern.

The trunk, he explains, contains letters, documents, and confidential records about the patriots' military stores. Even more important are the lists of those active in the cause of freedom. Should the British find the trunk, it could mean arrest, if not death, for many Americans. The enemy must not capture this prize. Will Lowell return at once and carry the trunk to the Reverend Mr. Clark's home? It should be safe enough there.

The secretary jumps out of the carriage, and Paul Revere volunteers to return with Lowell. The trunk is probably heavy, and the young man will need help in carrying it over to the parsonage.

As the two men walk back toward Lexington, the first streaks of a gray dawn appear on the eastern horizon. The bell in the little wooden belfry on the common is still tolling. Young William Diamond is beating a steady tattoo on his drum, summoning the minutemen to form ranks. Already the farmers and their sons, a pitifully thin line of determined patriots, are taking their places on Lexington Common.

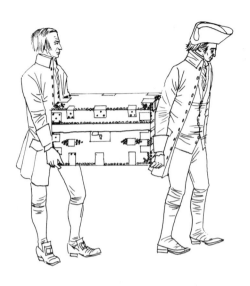

Lowell and Revere turn into Buckman
Tavern and mount the steps two at a time.
They find the precious trunk, still safe in
Lowell's room on the second floor. Glancing
out of the window, Revere catches sight of
several hundred redcoats approaching along
the winding road toward the Lexington green.
There's a glint of steel bayonets as the well-
trained army marches forward in rhythmical
step, their scarlet and gold uniforms shim-
mering in the first rays of the early morning
sun.

Paul Revere wonders what the pathetic little band of minutemen can hope to accomplish against this oncoming army. He would like to join the patriots, to stand beside these gallant men as they face the enemy. But his duty, at this moment, is to rescue Mr. Hancock's trunk.

Lowell and Revere grasp the trunk by its rope handles and hasten down the stairway. As they walk rapidly across the Common, the two men pass through the patriot lines. And they hear Captain Parker's now-famous warning:

DON'T FIRE UNLESS FIRED ON, BUT IF THEY MEAN TO HAVE A WAR LET IT BEGIN HERE.

Lugging the heavy trunk between them, Lowell and Revere hurry on toward the parsonage. A shot rings out. Revere turns his head, but his vision is obscured by a bush. He cannot determine who has fired the first shot; he can only see the British lines with smoke billowing up in front of them. The redcoats give "a great shout"; they rush forward, and there's the loud report of gunfire.

It is an awesome moment. The first shot of the American Revolution has just been fired. This means WAR! Revere feels pride for the part he has played in alerting the countryside. The colonists are well prepared. There may be many months, perhaps years, of fighting ahead. But Paul Revere is undaunted. The cause of liberty and freedom in America is worth whatever price the colonists must pay!

Bibliography

ALDEN, JOHN RICHARD. *The American Revolution.*
New York: Harper & Brothers, 1954.

ALDERMAN, CLIFFORD LINDSEY. *Samuel Adams, Son
of Liberty.* New York: Holt, Rinehart and Win-
ston, Inc., 1961.

BAKELESS, JOHN. *Turncoats, Traitors and Heroes.*
Philadelphia: J. B. Lippincott Company, 1959.

BAKELESS, KATHERINE and JOHN. *Spies of the Revolution.* Philadelphia: J. B. Lippincott Company,
1962.

BEEBE, LUCIUS M. *Boston and the Boston Legend.*
New York: D. Appleton-Century Company, 1935.

BIGELOW, FRANCIS HILL. *Historic Silver of the Colonies and Its Makers.* New York: Tudor Publishing Company, 1948.

BOWEN, CATHERINE DRINKER. *John Adams and the American Revolution*. Boston: Little, Brown and Company, 1950.

BRITT, ALBERT. *The Hungry War: An Account of the American Revolution*. Barre, Massachusetts: Barre Publishing Company, 1961.

COBURN, FRANK WARREN. *The Battle of April 19, 1775, in Lexington, Concord, Lincoln, Arlington, Cambridge, Somerville and Charlestown, Massachusetts*. Lexington, Massachusetts: published by the author, 1912.

CRAWFORD, MARY CAROLINE. *Old Boston in Colonial Days*. Boston: The Page Company, 1908.

FORBES, ESTHER. *The Boston Book*. Boston: Houghton Mifflin Company, 1947.

―――. *Johnny Tremain*. Cambridge, Massachusetts: The Riverside Press, 1943.

―――. *Paul Revere and the World He Lived In*. Cambridge, Massachusetts: The Riverside Press, 1942.

FRENCH, ALLEN. *The First Year of the American Revolution*. Boston: Houghton Mifflin Company, 1934.

GOSS, ELBRIDGE HENRY. *Life of Colonel Paul Revere*. 2 volumes. Boston: Howard W. Spare, Publisher, 1898.

HUDSON, CHARLES. *History of the Town of Lexington, From Its First Settlement to 1868*. Boston: Houghton Mifflin Company, 1913.

JENNINGS, JOHN. *Boston, Cradle of Liberty, 1650–*

1776. New York: Doubleday & Co., Inc., 1947.

LANCASTER, BRUCE. *From Lexington to Liberty*. New York: Doubleday & Co., Inc., 1955.

LANGDON, WILLIAM CHAUNCY. *Everyday Things in American Life, 1607–1776*. New York: Charles Scribner's Sons, 1955.

MILLER, JOHN C. *Origins of the American Revolution*. Boston: Little, Brown and Company, 1943.

REVERE, PAUL. "Letter to the Corresponding Secretary." Massachusetts Historical Society *Collections*, Vol. 5, pp. 106–112.

————. "Letter of Paul Revere to Dr. Belknap." Massachusetts Historical Society *Proceedings*, Vol. 16, pp. 371–376.

SCHEER, GEORGE F., and RANKIN, HUGH F. *Rebels and Redcoats*. New York: World Publishing Company, 1957.

SCUDDER, TOWNSEND. *Concord: American Town*. Boston: Little, Brown and Company, 1947.

SINGLETON, ESTHER. *Historic Buildings of America*. New York: Dodd, Mead & Co., 1907.

TOURTELLOT, ARTHUR BERNON. *The Charles*. New York: Farrar and Rinehart, 1941.

————. *William Diamond's Drum: The Beginning of the War of the American Revolution*. New York: Doubleday & Co., Inc., 1959.

WESTON, GEORGE F., JR. *Boston Ways: High, By, and Folk*. Boston: Beacon Press, 1957.

Index

Index

Acton, Mass., 45
Adams, Samuel, 9, 10,
    12, 34, 38, 42-46
    pass., 56, 58, 62, 69,
    79, 92, 94, 95, 98,
    114, 115
    and Revere, 97
American Revolution,
    first shot of, 119
Arlington Center, Mass.,
    89

Baker, John, 3
Ballard, John, 50
Barrett, James, Col., 34,
    44, 45
Beacon Hill, 4

Beaver, 11
Bedford, Mass., 41, 45
Bentley, Joseph, 37, 70,
    71, 72, 73, 76
Boston, 1, 17, 21, 46, 49
    British soldiers quar-
    tered in, 16, 17-18,
    24-25
    patriot activities in, 10
Boston Common, 18, 24,
    31, 52-53
Boston Harbor, 12, 13,
    16, 20, 21, 26
Boston Neck, 14, 16, 36,
    37, 46, 52, 56, 98
Boston Tea Party, 12-13
Brookline, Mass., 46
Brown, Capt., 29

127

Brown, Solomon, 93, 94, 95, 108

Buckman Tavern, 41, 96, 114, 115, 117

Cambridge, Mass., 47, 52, 55, 56, 62, 63, 72, 81, 85, 97, 111

Canton, Mass., 45

Charles River, 36, 47, 58, 64, 70, 78, 97

Charlestown, Mass., 37, 38, 40, 45, 46, 47, 54, 58, 62-66 pass., 72, 77, 97

Christ Church, 24, 46, 47, 53, 56, 58, 60, 61, 63, 65, 66, 77

Clark, Jonas, Rev., 33, 42, 43, 79, 94-97 pass., 99, 107, 113, 115

Clark, Mrs. Jonas, 42, 99, 101

Clark's Wharf, 1

Committee of Safety, 16, 78

Committee of Thirty, 26, 29

Conant, William, Col.,
37, 38, 40, 45, 46, 47, 56, 58, 63, 66, 76, 78, 80, 81

Concord, Mass., 29, 30, 32, 34, 41, 43, 45, 48, 52, 55, 88, 97, 99, 101, 103

Continental Congress, Second, 34, 42, 98, 114

Cooper Tavern, 89

Dartmouth, 11

Dawes, William, 56, 97, 98, 99, 102, 103, 104

deBerniere, Ensign, 29

Devens, Richard, 78, 79, 84

Diamond, William, 116

Eleanor, 11

Erving, Capt., 22

Fish Street, 2, 11, 21, 50

French and Indian War, 6

Gage, Thomas, Gen., 16, 18, 27-30 pass., 33, 34, 36, 49, 55, 68, 93

George III, 6, 7, 8, 16, 21
Green Dragon Tavern,
    19, 22, 26, 28, 31
grenadiers, British, 30

Hall, Isaac, Capt., 88
Hancock, John, 10, 12,
    33, 34, 38, 42-46
    pass., 56, 58, 62, 69,
    79, 92, 94, 95, 98,
    113, 114, 115
    and Revere, 97, 115
Harvard College, 4

Jasper (gunsmith), 53

Lancaster, Mass., 45
Larkin, John, Deacon,
    80, 111
Lexington, Mass., 33, 40,
    42, 48, 52, 55, 56,
    62, 64, 69, 70, 79-86
    pass., 89, 92, 94, 97,
    98, 99, 113
Lexington Common, 41,
    43, 109, 113, 114,
    116, 118
light infantry, British, 30
Lincoln, Mass., 95
Lively, 13

Loring, Jonathan, 95,
    108
Lowell, John, 114-118
    pass.

Maryland, 17
Massachusetts Bay Col-
    ony, 10, 17, 18
Massachusetts General
    Court, 33
Medford, Mass., 88, 89
Middlesex County,
    Mass., 80, 89
minutemen, 19, 28, 46,
    48, 88, 90, 94, 116,
    118
Mitchell, Edward, Maj.,
    107, 108, 109, 111
Mulliken, Lydia, 103
Mulliken, Nathaniel,
    103
Munroe, William, Sgt.,
    94, 96, 98, 115
Munroe's Tavern, 94
Mystic River, 88, 89

Newman, Robert, 47, 48,
    53, 54, 58-66 *pass.*,
    77
New York, 16

North Square, 22, 24, 25,
  65, 68, 69, 113

Parker, Capt., 118
Parliament, 7, 8, 25, 30
Philadelphia, 16, 34, 42,
  98, 114
Portsmouth, N. H., 28
Prescott, Samuel, Dr.,
  103, 104, 105
Provincial Congress, 33
Pulling, John, 61, 63, 64,
  65

Quartering Act, 25

Revere, Paul, 1, 2, 7, 9,
  11, 12, 16-22 *pass.*,
  25, 31, 32, 33, 47-70
  pass., 109, 111
  as dentist, 3-4
  as engraver, 3
  home of, 22
  near capture, 86-87
  questioned by British,
    105-107, 108
  rides of, 34-45 *pass.*,
    70-92 *pass.*, 96-104
  pass.

as silversmith, 1, 2
spy system organized
  by, 26-29, 31, 49
Revere, Rachel, 24, 25,
  69
Richardson, Tom, 70,
  71-72, 73, 76
Rivoire, Apollos, 2
Roxbury, Mass., 46, 56,
  99

Sanderson, Elijah, 95,
  108
Second Continental Con-
  gress, 34, 42, 98, 114
Somerset, 58, 62, 63, 72,
  73, 76, 78
Somerville, Mass., 81
Sons of Liberty, 9, 10,
  12, 26, 37, 48, 56,
  103
South Carolina, 17
Stamp Act, 7
Stedman, Mrs. John, 52

"taxation without repre-
  sentation," 7
Tories, 7, 10, 26

Warren, Joseph, Dr., 4, 10, 17, 19, 26, 27, 28, 31-36 *pass.*, 38, 42, 53, 55, 59, 62, 70, 97

Watson, Abraham, 78, 79

Whigs, 8

Woburn, Mass., 115

ABOUT THE AUTHOR

While Mary Kay Phelan was writing *Four Days in Philadelphia—1776,* which tells the story of the Second Continental Congress and the adoption of the Declaration of Independence, her attention was caught by Paul Revere. Though he was not a delegate to the Congress, Revere's friendship with fellow patriots, his activities as a member of the Sons of Liberty, and of course his famous ride, made him an important contributor to the Congress's success.

History has been both a vocation and an avocation for Mrs. Phelan. She does research for and edits 8-mm. historical movies, and in addition to *Four Days in Philadelphia* and *Midnight Alarm,* she has written three books in the Crowell Holiday series: *Mother's Day, The Fourth of July,* and *Election Day.* She was born in Baldwin City, Kansas, graduated from DePauw University in Indiana, and received her M.A. from Northwestern University. She lives with her family in Davenport, Iowa.

ABOUT THE ILLUSTRATOR

Leonard Weisgard's varied career spans many artistic fields. He has designed magazine covers, painted murals for Macy's, designed sets and costumes for the theater and ballet, and illustrated innumerable books for children.

Mr. Weisgard lives in Roxbury, Connecticut, with his wife and three children. As a parent he is active in support of school libraries, believing them to be the central core of all good schools.